PEARLS ALONG THE PATH

Lessons for Living A Life With Passion

PEARLS ALONG THE PATH

Lessons for Living A Life With Passion

 Ronald Paul Hill, Ph.D.

Pearls Along the Path
by Ronald Paul Hill, Ph.D.

Published in 1999

The quotes from Roosevelt, Kroc, Schweitzer, Disney, and Wooden come from Great Quotes From Great Leaders, Career Press, pages 11, 32, 35, 63, and 106, respectively. The Huxley quote is from Passages Journal, Running Press.

Text is set in Bembo; heads are set in Humana Sans. Book and cover design by Pete Masterson, Aeonix Publishing Group, http://www.aeonix.com.

00 99   0 9 8 7 6 5 4 3 2 1

Publisher's Cataloging–in–Publication
(Provided by Quality Books, Inc.)

Hill, Ronald Paul.
　　Pearls along the path : lessons for living a life with passion / by Ronald Paul Hill. -- 1st ed.
　　　　p. cm.
　　　　LCCN: 99–61698
　　　　ISBN: 0-9652615-0-6

　　　1. Personnel management.   2. Organizational effectiveness.   3. Performance.   4. Success in business   5. Interpersonal relations   I. Title.

HF5549.H55 1999　　　　　　　 658.3'14
　　　　　　　　　　　　　　　 QBI99-511

Published by:
Bialkin Books, 25381 Alicia Parkway #G-336, Laguna Hills, CA 92653
Printed in Canada

Dedication

This book is dedicated to the men, women, and children whose lives have touched mine. Especially Noel, Paul, and PJ.

Contents

*E*xperience is not what happens to you; it is what you do with what happens to you.

—Aldous Huxley

The Importance of These Lessons

This book was written at the urging of colleagues, clients, and former students. It is about a personal journey and the pearls of wisdom I collected as I travelled the path of my life. I strung these pearls together to create a series of seminars, and these seminars were the outline for this book. Now I can share my accumulated wisdom with many more people.

Although I have been a teacher for most of my life, I continue to be a student as well. My teaching career began in 1970 as a martial arts and physical fitness instructor and, six years later, I became a university faculty member. Working with tens of thousands of young people, business executives, and colleagues led me to reflect on the lives of those around me as well as my own life.

What I learned was at times painful, at times exciting, but all were integral to who I am today. Something would occur to heighten my awareness: a conversation, the death of a loved one; some event, usually tragic, to which I could do little more than react. How much easier if those lessons crystallized at once, like a flash of lightning.

I struggled to understand each event. Was it related to something in my life, or was it a powerful directing force? A lesson would sometimes contradict the beliefs and attitudes I acquired from my parents and siblings. This struggle was particularly painful: If I couldn't trust my family, whom could I trust?

Part 1 is where the path begins... with childhood experiences.

In Part 2 the path turns, then turns again, and I discover more pearls beneath roadside bushes— my school and early work experiences. These pearls are multicolored, some with the blush of excitement and joy, others dark with envy.

In Part 3, I may appear to retrace some steps, turning back to early teenage years before going forward. That is because we don't learn all of life's lessons immediately. Some things become clear only from a distance or when linked with other meaningful experiences.

In Part 4, I examine aspects of love and marriage that emerged from my experiences with a variety of people in diverse circumstances.

I sincerely hope that the pearls I offer here will help you learn more easily the wisdom from pearls you pluck from your own path.

Part 1: Early Lessons

The quality of an individual is reflected in the standards they set for themselves.

—Ray Kroc

Part 1: Early Lessons

Chapter 1

Being Tough

When I was thirteen, my family moved from Louisville, Kentucky to outside Washington, DC. I felt disconnected for months as I grappled with the loss of my friends. Over time, I made new friends but it wasn't until I began martial arts training that I found a guiding influence for my life. The "centering" it provided made everything else, including schoolwork, easier to understand and do.

By age 17, I earned a karate black belt, and decided to push my physical conditioning further through weight training. I continued this routine during college with a weight lifting course, and followed it with a three-times-a-week program at the local YMCA. Eventually I could bench press 250 pounds, which was impressive for a young man who weighed 175 pounds. But my pride was dashed the day Johnny Woods reappeared.

The scrawny kid I had known in elementary school now stood five foot eight, still shorter than me, but he was a 200-pound muscle man who could bench press a whopping 400-pounds. There wasn't one weight lifting exercise where I could match him. The machismo in me tried to dismiss his achievement: "He only lifts weights while I do martial arts training as well!" It didn't work. The image of Johnny Woods would affect me for most of my life.

A few years later, a shattered thumb joint kept me from competing in a national karate championship. I went to the championship eager to watch the "who's who" of invited masters. I entered the gym thinking that I was in their "league" but soon had my illusions shattered. One-by-one, the invited champions overwhelmed their regional rivals with such ease that they almost made fools of them. Didn't I perform the same moves as these champions? Then why did their techniques look so much different and better?

After the event, I commiserated with a close friend who had been in the ring with these superhuman creatures. "What are we doing wrong?" I asked. "How can we correct our deficiencies?"

Mike had the same questions; neither of us had answers. Then we had an idea. "Let's ask one of these superstars to take us on as students. Once they see our sincere desire to learn and our innate ability, they will surely accept us!"

As two of the four finalists lived nearby, we decided to approach the one who seemed friendlier and less egotistic. But first we spent several days converting Mike's basement into a karate dojo, a large empty space except for a mat. Then, when we were certain that our new *sensei* (teacher) would be impressed, we made the call.

Our champion was not only interested, he offered to bring one of his students to help him gauge our abilities. The two of us took turns sparring with this young man. I held my own, but Mike was less confident and chose not to seek additional lessons. Over the next several months, I spent many hours as a human punching bag. One day the *sensei* knocked me into the corner of the dojo; I smashed into a picture of their founding instructor and broken glass scattered everywhere. The result was a massive headache and a decision not to return.

It was Johnny all over again. I was good but not great, and I wanted to be great. What was left? Academia. Now there was a place I excelled!

It worked. During my first few years in college I was admitted to all the honor societies offered by my university, including the prestigious business honor society of Beta Gamma Sigma. The marketing faculty nominated me for "top undergraduate marketing student in the city." I won this honor, along with a scholarship for my final undergraduate year. Yes, I was tops in education!

I was on the fast track to greatness, which was about to end abruptly. After graduation I accepted a position at a local consulting firm. I saw this job as the first lap of a journey in which I was destined to make my mark on the world. But it was not long before I discovered that I was the only new hire who lacked an MBA degree from a top school such as Harvard or Wharton. Everyone else not only had more education but better credentials than I did. Muscle man Johnny all over again!

I took my misery to the YMCA gym, hoping to forget for a time this newly discovered deficiency. I was pressing weights when Johnny, who I had not seen for some time, strolled in. I greeted him and asked him where he had been.

"In jail. It was the worst time in my life," he said.

"Well, at least you were able to stay in shape! You look as good or better than you ever have!"

He said, "Yeah, I trained hard, but the guys I was with put me to shame. *Being tough* depends on who's in the room at the time."

I was dumbfounded. If Johnny could be topped, was anyone safe? What about my karate champion? He had come in third. And all those MBAs at the office... they all couldn't have been at the top of their classes.

I felt as if I had been holding my breath for years. Now I let it out slowly, as I reexamined every aspect of my life: lifting weights, practicing martial arts, studying hard. I wasn't happy with my performance when I realized I wasn't the best. Now I wondered: Did I have to strive to be the best when being the best wasn't possible? If being the best depends on who is in the room at the time, could I learn to enjoy these things regardless of who is in the room?

I turned a corner then, thanks to Johnny, but I wasn't entirely cured of the need to be the best. A former karate student of mine became the instructor to several football players at a local university, and he invited me to their first belt promotion. When I was surrounded by these five young men, each of whom was 250 to 300 pounds of pure muscle, each eager to shake the tiny hand of their instructor's master, I was overwhelmed. Are we even the same species?

I remembered a line from one of Clint Eastwood's movies, "A man's got to know his limitations." Suddenly I saw another meaning to this sentence. Many people fail to make an effort. They don't try to succeed because of self-imposed limitations. Regardless of my own limits, I vowed never to admit defeat by failing to try.

Some years later, the final piece of that puzzle fell into place. Then Beth Hirschman, a professional colleague, and I were at a coffee shop, relaxing after a long day spent at an international conference. I mused aloud about a particularly boring speaker, "Why did so-and-so get an endowed chair at a prestigious university when my record is better than his?"

Beth looked sympathetically at me. "Ron, you can't just look at one aspect of the man's life and wish to exchange. Are you willing to trade everything with him?"

The answer came quickly: "My university was not as highly regarded as his, but it was in a nicer location. The dean, my colleagues, and my students valued my work, and I was successful there. I preferred my research areas as well as the student body at my university. I had a successful marriage, whereas he was recently been divorced. My life was not perfect, but it was pretty good. I was happy.

Comparisons can rob us of the energy to do our best. We begin our negative comparisons in childhood when we compete for our parents' attention with our siblings. At school, we compare ourselves by the grades teachers assign us; at work, we compare ourselves by the raises and promotions we receive based on our performance. When a teacher praises a student for the "best" paper, or a raise is granted for having top sales, what does this say to the rest? Are they all losers?

This comparison mind-set seeps into every aspect of our lives. The award for "salesperson of the month" goes to the one with the highest sales. The homecoming queen is the one with the most votes. The rest, unfortunately, are discarded like yesterday's newspaper. Even the runners-up in the Super Bowl and the World Series suffer public humiliation following their loss.

More tragic is that such comparisons begin so early in life that we learn to do it to ourselves. For example, most women in this country are unhappy with at least some part of their physical appearance. Why? Because they compare themselves to the micro-thin, long-legged, large-breasted mutant models paraded in the media!

We should not avoid all comparisons, however; some have value. When we gauge our success against the success of others, we have a reality check of our performance (not ability) which helps us set goals for future achievement.

Such goals need not be realistic. Most children who participate in Little League dream of becoming big league players when they mature. Fantasies like this give us permission to reach beyond the ordinary. Tiger Woods exemplifies this process. His childhood dreams, as much as his talent, attest to the power of positive, self-fulfilling prophesies.

There is a place and a value for comparisons to direct the behavior and effort of young people. Consider the "everything is excellent!" baby-boomer mentality of noncompetitive sports that poses a danger to our children. I saw this in action when I helped coach my son's T-ball (pre-baseball) team. The head coach asked us never to mention the score of a game. Instead, we were to emphasize teamwork and self-esteem. Despite my misgivings, I went along with his instructions. But, when a young player tossed the ball in the wrong direction and the coach shouted "Good throw!" I recognized the underlying problem.

Praise-for-anything can defeat the goal of building skills. It will not prepare them for higher-level play, and it won't prepare them for the realities of the adult world.

Yet praise-for-anything is not as destructive to our development as the multitude of negative comparisons. When negative comparisons swamp the positive, we may lose the confidence to try. "Why bother dieting when I'll never look like Cindy Crawford?" or, "I can't believe I missed being salesperson of the month by $2000 again. I might as well give up!"

The result may be that we take fewer personal and professional risks and become increasingly bitter and isolated from those around us.

So, how do we deal with this problem? We can recognize when negative comparisons occur by learning to detect the inner signals that tell us we are sabotaging our sense of self-worth. It begins with awareness of when we make a negative comparison. Awareness commences when we get an unpleasant sensation such as anxiety, or have a negative thought such as, "I feel fat." Or it may surface as office gossip when we disparage a successful colleague.

The next step involves uncovering the reasons behind our feelings. Have you ever asked yourself why you dislike a successful colleague, or feel belittled when others are praised and you are not? Where does the negative comparison stem from? Is it self-imposed? Is it externally imposed by teachers, coaches, or bosses?

Then we need to ask, "How valid is this comparison?" Start by asking if this comparison is relevant to your important life pursuits. If so, should you expect yourself to perform at the same level as this other person? If the answer to either of these questions is "no," tell yourself that the comparison is inappropriate. Armed with this new insight, you can refuse to allow such comparisons to erode your self-esteem simply by seeing them for what they are... invalid.

On the other hand, if the comparison is valid and does matter, we need to put it to good use. Turn this negative comparison into a positive by taking steps to overcome the realistic deficiency, such as additional education or training.

The best way to start is with small steps and small challenges. Long-term, larger goals are more difficult, and call for courage and determination (*e.g.,* "I will lose 25 pounds this year.") Such courage offers freedom to make the most of our lives. When we do, we internalize the comparisons from others and begin to measure our personal development as self-improvement rather than as an unending competition.

Unending competition is a losing game: We can always find someone who is stronger, thinner, smarter, faster, or wealthier. "Being tough depends on who is in the room at the time." We can always find someone in our room to make us unhappy with ourselves!

Chapter 2

Parents and Unconditional Love

My mother, Dolores, was a petite, olive-skinned beauty with dark curly hair and fiery brown eyes. Her charm and grace were evident not only to her contemporaries, but also my friends who often stopped to chat with her, sometimes at length, before they turned to me. These conversations covered every possible topic—from girlfriends to school to jobs to relationships with their parents. They knew they could confide in her and receive adult advice without judgment. Many of them called her "mom," suggesting the nature of their deep personal relationship with her.

Within the family, our daily lives were organized by Mom's efforts within our home. She was the primary source of nurturing and adult wisdom for all the children. Equally important, each of my siblings—older and younger brothers and two younger sisters—had an independent and intimate relationship with her. The first memory to come to mind is the countless times I returned from school, sat down at the dining room table and shared an after-school snack and the day's events with Mom. She always listened carefully, provided guidance when necessary, and taught me the value and virtue of personal integrity.

On July 6, 1974, after six months of suffering, Mom succumbed to cancer. Her death devastated my family. We felt cast adrift. For several years after her sudden death we struggled mightily. Our schoolwork suffered, our friendships seemed less important. Unable to find a reason for her premature demise, we rebelled against our religious upbringing. Each of us suffered alone. Mom was the glue that held us together; it was years before we were comfortable talking to one another about the meaning of this tragic event in our lives.

As our grief diminished, we began to share stories about her that, in retrospect, seemed rather silly. My younger brother, Phillip, remembered the last time Mom got mad at him and sent him for a belt so that she could smack his behind. At the time, he was already several inches taller than she was, and he returned with a wimpy, dilapidated cloth belt for her to use and a silver plate stuffed in his shorts for "protection." We all howled at the memory and my mother's frustration that we were getting too old to be disciplined like children.

Through this sharing of personal recollections we realized that each of us was convinced that he or she was her favorite. This allowed us to pursue our diverse interests without the need to compete for her love and approval. Mom's love and approval were there for each of us, unconditionally.

This unconditional love and approval became the foundation upon which I began to actualize my potential so that, even as a relatively young man, I was good at sports, earned top grades, and maintained solid friendships with my peers. It was a bedrock that carried me until postgraduate school.

Everyone in the Ph.D. program was bright and motivated to succeed. Competition, combined with the amount and content of the course work, made it the most challenging period of my academic life. I did well, but my experience with one professor helped clarify my understanding of unconditional love.

Dr. Ford was "under the gun" in his own job due to escalating expectations from a business school on the rise to publish articles. With his considerable research skills and solid work ethic, he was just beginning to experience professional triumphs. He freely passed on to us his insights about what was needed to be successful within academia, and articulated the standards for research and teaching that we would need to be effectual by national standards.

I wanted to do well in his course for a number of reasons. Not only was it the basic research course but it laid the foundation for success in the university community. In year two of the program, the faculty would decide whether I was capable of doctoral level study or should exit the program with an MBA. And, Dr. Ford and I shared many of the same characteristics (Catholic, athletic, hard working, etc.). Also, I wanted to impress him.

I studied diligently at first and tried to dazzle him with my comprehension of the material. When I saw that he was "underwhelmed" by my performance, I skipped spring vacation and worked 10 hours a day on the take-home midterm exam. I received an "A" for this effort; successful, I thought, until I saw Dr. Ford's reaction to my term paper.

I'd chosen to investigate AT&T because Dr. Ford was interested in the telecommunications industry. I gathered as much material as I could find, and conferred with my uncle and his associates who worked for the firm. After several grueling days of writing, I eagerly delivered what I believed to be a strong paper.

It was returned with a "B" grade and only a few words written in Dr. Ford's hand: "Too pro-AT&T." Apparently, he did not think the paper was worthy of discussion or debate, and certainly not praise. Dejected and filled with self-pity, I vowed to challenge him.

By the time we met the following week, I was angry. I confronted him about all the long hours spent, the phone conversations with AT&T executives, etc. How dare he dismiss all my hard work with so little reaction and such a modest grade? He looked at me directly and quietly said, "Nobody pays for input; everybody pays for output."

Instantly, I remembered the T-ball coach shouting, "Good toss!" when the player threw the ball the wrong direction. Had my mother's unconditional acceptance, combined with my earlier and easier successes, lulled me into complacency? Dr. Ford's quiet words thrust me into the realities of competing in the adult world.

It was not the last time I would experience this lesson. I am reminded of the lesson each time a student demands, "How could you give me a 'D' on this project after I spent three full weeks writing it? This grade is so unfair!"

"Well, let's look at it from my perspective," I reply. "Should I judge your work on its quality or the amount of effort expended?" I usually end the conversation with, *"Only your parents love you unconditionally; everyone else expects you to perform."*

Many students are confused by this statement. They confuse input for output, and continue to insist that they performed well. At this point I ask them to make a simple consumer choice: "Which one of these two products would you choose if both are offered at the same price? The first is made by European craftspersons and took two years to finish, but it only meets half of your important needs for this good. The other comes from Japan, was assembled in four weeks, and meets all of your needs." The answer is obvious, but few students want to think of themselves as a commodity subject to such an evaluation!

The most difficult example of this came from coaching my eldest son Paul, who had played baseball for five years. Paul was an outstanding athlete who responded quickly to positive suggestions. By the time he was ten, I thought it best to give him the opportunity to learn from someone more knowledgeable about baseball than I. We talked about the pluses and minuses of this change, and we concluded that he was ready to go on without me.

He tried out for the highest-level league for his age group in our community, and he was drafted by one of the coaches. However, he had difficulty connecting with the ball when he was at bat, and these failures resulted in his taking fewer chances and swinging less. His coach noted his reluctance as well as poor performance, and he began playing Paul less and less.

Paul became increasingly frustrated. He would ask me angrily after each game: "Why doesn't coach play me more often? I come to every practice, but he pulls me out of the game and plays other guys who rarely show up or come late!" I realized that Paul was confusing input and output just as I had.

But I waited until our next postgame discussion when he posed his usual question. This time I said, "Son, I love you no matter what you do on the field, but your coach is not your father. He wants to win games and won't play you unless you are the best person for a particular position." Paul burst out with a series of excuses for his failure to hit the ball. We were going nowhere.

I tried a different approach. I asked him how many outs he had while playing first base during this game. He told me, "Four, with one error." I asked what he thought of that performance. He was pleased, he said, especially with the fourth out, as the ball was thrown over his head. I agreed with this assessment, but followed with a similar question involving his experience at the plate.

Framed within the context of his positive performance, Paul was able to be more critical of his batting. He had struck out twice and only swung at two balls. He recognized his output as unsatisfactory, and vowed to work to achieve a higher level of performance. And Paul did improve. Paul was no more than ten but many individuals far older continue to think they are entitled to unconditional acceptance.

I once accepted an administrative job, replacing a person who had the choice of reporting to me or resigning. He agreed to report to me but in our initial discussion of his new job responsibilities, he told me in no uncertain terms that he expected to be treated "better" than the other employees. By virtue of his thirty years as an administrator, he expected to be excused from the more mundane parts of his job, and to receive the highest pay and most benefits among his peers. Pretty good work if you can get it!

Once again, the lesson is deceptively simple. Many of us were fortunate to have parents who loved us unconditionally. This nurturing foundation allowed us to move out into the larger world with less fear and more confidence in our abilities. Yet, we may mistakenly use this premise to measure our worth in other relationships, especially work and professional ones. Our parents may have asked little from us in return for their affection and appreciation, but most people expect us to perform!

I recognize that all relationships have some personal dimension. From marriage to our friendships at work, some level of commitment applies. Central to all is the responsibility to meet certain expectations associated with our role. Input (what you do) is a necessary ingredient, but it is not enough on its own. Output (how well you perform) is also required.

To apply this lesson, I often step back from current relationships to examine them. To what extent is each relationship based on input versus output? If output standards are essential to success, what are those standards? Students, colleagues, and clients who grapple with these critical questions often see their professional and personal associations in a new light.

This relationship analysis can reduce our frustration levels. A research project that examined the loss of a major account revealed that salespersons often felt betrayed by customers, and they compare this loss to divorce. This may seem to be an exaggeration, but such a loss may have an impact on their friendships, status at work, incomes, and marital relationships.

When I focus on output expectations in personal and professional relationships, the loss holds a different meaning. In these circumstances, I can see these associations for what they provide. I am also free to consider my needs in these relationships, and determine if what I must to do to satisfy others is warranted by what they offer in exchange.

Part 2: On Ability and Performance

Don't measure yourself by what you have accomplished, but by what you should have accomplished with your ability.

—John Wooden

Part 2: On Ability and Performance

Chapter 3

Ability-Performance Nexus

I entered first grade as a five-year-old. Maybe it was because I'd barely made the age cutoff, but I performed poorly, according to the standards of the day. Although my grades were marginal from one year to the next, I was passed forward albeit grudgingly by my teachers.

The wake-up call came in fifth grade. Mom returned from meeting with my teacher and looked at me with concern, but said everything was fine. Later, when she thought she was alone with my father, she gave him a different and more accurate picture of the conference. The teacher said my performance for the year was below expectations, and showed my mother several examples of my low-quality work. Mom had seen this before, even expected it, but was surprised with my teacher's reaction.

Mom told how the teacher noted my scores on several standardized exams, including the "IQ" test, then compared me to her own son. Our scores were nearly equal, yet he was at the top of our class. Why, she asked my mother, was I failing to live up to my ability?

My parents talked freely, unaware that I was eavesdropping. I felt ashamed and embarrassed. Was I really doing something wrong?

By the time I was in junior high school, the discipline of martial arts and the guidance of early mentors became the catalysts I needed to pursue my studies passionately. I moved quickly to the top of the class, and felt capable of accomplishing any and all academic tasks.

The next exposure to this lesson came in high school. I was performing some menial cleaning tasks in the cafeteria with a fellow student. We had known each other for about two years, but were not friends. As we worked, we made small talk. Eventually we talked about our performance in school.

He asked (in an almost defensive tone), "Why do you study so hard? Who are you trying to impress?" He further noted that "I am at least as bright as you, but my motto is 'I don't GAF' (give a f___)."

I think he expected me to be impressed by his apathy, but I responded: "If that's true, I feel sorry for you. What a waste. What good is ability that is never used?"

Suddenly I heard the alarm from the wake-up call that came the day I overheard my parents discussing my ability-performance connection. I now was determined to make the most of life by using my God-given talents to the best of my ability.

Another vivid reminder of this lesson came from a comparison of my own adult life to that of Jack Kaslo. A bright and outgoing young man, Jack was one of my best friends throughout junior and senior high school. He also was a pretty good student, which made us friendly rivals. One day he asked me what my IQ score was. To our surprise, our scores were identical!

After high school, Jack and I went to different universities. I later learned that he was experimenting with the hallucinogenic drug, LSD. He returned home after his sophomore year in the middle of a psychotic episode. Several months passed before Jack was able to function normally. But he was not cured. For the next several years, Jack was in and out of several different programs of study as he fought mental illness. Eventually, he became homeless. He never married, had children, or held a fulfilling job.

I have thought of Jack often over the last twenty years. Why did this happen to him? If we had the same level of intelligence, why didn't it happen to me? Jack, more than anyone else I have known, represents the highest-level-of-ability/lowest-level-of-performance nexus. This is a frightening vision for any concerned friend, parent, or employer.

After years of reflection on these as well as other incidents, I resolved my feelings on the ability–performance nexus by seeking excellence in the activities I choose to pursue. I ask my students, children, colleagues, and clients to do the same, but usually meet with considerable resistance. Students tell me that they are dropping out of the business or accounting program because "I can't pass math" or "Economics is too hard."

On further probing, I often find that one professor or course challenged their abilities beyond their comfort zone. Then I ask the student to consider two questions: Is this an ability problem ("I can't do it"), or a performance problem ("It is hard to do")? If it's a performance problem ("doable"), what are the costs of not trying?

In this light, some students recognize that the short-run pain of successfully completing a difficult course is worth the long-run gain of a thirty-year career!

Negative thinking is not limited to students or young people. I remember a conversation I heard between several tenured faculty members at my university. They complained they would never become good scholars because our school required too much teaching and had fewer resources than a nationally ranked university in our community. I commented that several of our colleagues had developed stellar academic reputations under the same constraints. Did those successful peers have more ability or did the complainers fail to perform up their potential?

No one likes to be challenged with the message: "Failure may be the result of not working hard enough to make my desires come true." My university colleagues certainly did not! Yet, how can we explain different performance levels among equally trained individuals (i.e., Ph.D. in business administration) given equal resources?

Of course, a host of other factors may have an impact on one's performance, especially personal factors such as physical and mental health. But why do organizations experience such variation in performance levels among employees when they work so hard to recruit people with similar abilities for the same occupation? My contention is that few among us truly understand the ability-performance nexus as it relates to our own life pursuits.

To make this lesson valuable to me, I examined my own ability-performance nexus. "What talents/skills do I bring to the critical roles in my life? How well am I using them?" I've often heard a left-handed compliment about persons of (presumably) high potential who fail to make it: "She or he had good training." It's like hearing your blind date has a "good personality." The fact is, training alone is insufficient. The concentrated application of ability to relevant tasks is what makes one perform successfully.

Woody Allen once noted that "Ninety percent of life [involves] showing up." My experience suggests that hard and focused effort must follow. Of course, there will always be roadblocks such as resource constraints, political infighting, personal problems, etc. But the true success stories, the individuals who thrive regardless of conditions around them, are the ones who do not allow their focus and energy to be sidetracked from their ultimate goal of *actualizing their ability-performance nexus.*

Part 2: On Ability and Performance

Chapter 4

Passion In Work

There is nothing in the world quite like new love! (Notice I didn't say young love.) My wife and I often reminisce about the early days of our relationship when we couldn't be apart for more than a few hours without missing each other. These relationships are all consuming, energizing, and unforgettable.

For most of us, however, these experiences are rare, coming only once or twice in a lifetime, and they are part of a very limited domain within our lives. Our brush with passionate feelings may have occurred long ago, when we were younger and more willing to open ourselves to new experiences. Few aspects of our lives may ever contain passion. Instead, we experience thrilling highs vicariously, through the lives of celebrities or characters in movies or books.

I feel fortunate because passion has been an integral part of my life: I am passionate about learning, teaching, research, community service, and public speaking. Athletic competitions (as competitor or coach) are incredibly energizing, and they have sustained my enthusiasm for exercise my entire adult life. I still feel passionate about my wife and my children, and we work together to fill our lives with exciting and stimulating events.

Real passion in my life began with martial arts training. My decision to take karate lessons was prompted by an altercation with a local bully. I'd actually been the victor, but he vowed to get even with me the next time our paths crossed. Knowing he had more friends and they were better street fighters than I, made me determined to protect myself adequately.

I'd heard the stories that make up martial arts folklore — about secret techniques conceived thousands of years ago by Asian warriors and ninjas which could immobilize an opponent by the slightest touch to a pressure point. If only I could learn their secrets! I was unaware that untold hours of rigorous physical conditioning were required before I could master even the essential techniques.

Initial training went slowly. I marveled at the speed and dexterity of the advanced students as I watched them perform complex movements. Every technique or *kata* (series of techniques) that my instructors revealed was a rare jewel to be coveted, and the dance-like beauty inherent in each of them mesmerized. I celebrated my progression in ability/ performance as I moved from one color belt to the next, and spent countless hours with fellow students inside as well as outside the dojo.

By the time I passed the black belt exam, I was completely absorbed by the sport. Virtually every important aspect of my life was now connected to martial arts participation, from my love interest to income as an instructor, and I spent most of my free time thinking, doing, and talking about karate. If passion can be defined outside of love relationships, I was passionate!

The passion I am talking about is not obsession. It shares some of the same characteristics, including the ability to be completely absorbing. However, as I use it here, passion is a positive influence, a source of great personal joy and an inspiration to seek more from life.

One of the most passionate aspects of my professional life is academic research. When I completed the doctoral course work, I was unsure about the topic to pursue for my dissertation. Fortunately, I'd met Jim Glass, a professor in government and politics at my university. Jim was involved in fascinating work involving the application of complex psychological and psychiatric theories to political thinking. (Not a stretch if you think about how our government often operates!) His work and the readings he assigned were enthralling, and I used this theoretical base as the primary focus for a dissertation on consumer behavior.

Once I completed this, graduated, and took my first job as a professor, I had difficulty publishing my research. It didn't fit neatly into any category of scholarship that was popular in the field at the time. Given that long-term tenure at a university depends on successful publication, I wondered if I should select a new area to pursue, one more acceptable to my peers. Or should I throw caution to the wind and follow my passion?

One day, at a meeting with MBA students during student office hours, we discussed the application of several theories to the consumer behavior of AIDS victims. It was a lively conversation and very topical for the time. As they were leaving my office, one student asked to speak with me privately. Chuck remained when the others left, and told me that he had been diagnosed as HIV-positive that morning. Then he sobbed uncontrollably on my shoulder.

I was stunned. I had recently begun applying my consumer-behavior and marketing training to the study of difficult social problems, but had only modest publication success. Now my work took on new meaning—there was a human face to what had been academic and political discussions. The process of examining, understanding, and possibly contributing to the debate of issues like AIDS was more important than individual success. I felt more passionate about and more committed to my research, and willing to take the risks necessary to pursue what I believed was important.

Over the next decade, I was unrelenting in the pursuit and evaluation of critical social issues from a consumer or marketing perspective. Whether political advertising, lobbying activities, homelessness, abortion, consumer debt, welfare reform, or spousal abuse, I forged my own path in the field. More importantly, I was successful because my passion energized me to make the most of my abilities.

As I moved from one issue to the next, I came in contact with the people most affected by these problems. In one instance, for the better part of a year I worked one afternoon a week at a shelter for homeless women and their children. I spoke with them, discussed how they managed to acquire enough food and clothing to survive, and often was overcome with feelings of great sadness.

I wish I could convince everyone of the pivotal role of passion in helping us actualize our ability-performance nexus. I have a close friend who is one of the brightest people I've ever known, yet he stays in a job that offers him little satisfaction, let alone passion. I asked him: "Why?"

He answered, "I've been working at it too long now to change. What do you want me to do: quit my job and open a store on the beach or write the Great American Novel?"

My response will always be: "Yes, if those things would bring passion to your life!"

My students, at both the graduate and undergraduate levels, do not fare much better. Occasionally one says, "I don't really like accounting (or marketing, human resources, etc.), but I majored in it because I know I'll get a job that pays well."

I nod my head at this lunacy and reply, "I would rather drive a ten-year old Dodge to a job that I am passionate about than drive a brand new Lexus to one that I am not."

They often retort, "I will find passion in other parts of my life!"

"Maybe so," I assert, "but if you're willing to compromise your entire career, how can you be certain you won't sell yourself short elsewhere?"

Even those who are willing to listen to my tirade, may become confused. They ask, "How do we know which pursuits will give us sustained passion? How can we be sure that following our passions will provide a more fulfilling life?"

My answer to the first question: Find your own passions rather than share mine or anyone else's.

To the second: "If I asked you to run a mile at your top speed, how fast would you run? Now, how much faster would you run if you knew that your child was drowning in a lake located one mile from where you are standing?"

Clearly, the motivation to run the distance changes dramatically from the first to the second context, just as performance at a job changes when we become passionate about it.

To live life to the fullest, give yourself the freedom to pursue those things which bring passion to your life.

I am not advocating the total abdication of personal responsibility. Within the context of reasonable adult living (e.g., honoring commitments to others, having a place to live, paying the bills, etc.), we must give ourselves the luxury of seeking and finding employment opportunities that make us excited to go to work in the morning.

No one but you can determine what brings you passion. Passion, like beauty, is in "the eye of the beholder." However, a few simple and probing questions are a good starting point. I often ask students, "What businesses and industries cause you to feel passion? What professional opportunities exist within these areas?"

Your instant answer may be "Victoria's Secret." But take time to consider generic categories of goods and services such as sports, entertainment, travel, technology, charities, or a host of others which may fascinate you.

Some people say, "I've loved sports my whole life, but isn't it difficult to find a good job in that field?"

My response is "So what? Are you willing to give up your dream before you even try to fulfill it?"

Others tell me "I would love to work for that company, but the pay is too low."

Again, I remind them that doing things you love during most of your waking hours is worth the (opportunity) loss of income.

There are many success stories among students who have heeded this advice. Philip, who grew up near the Canadian border, played hockey with utter abandon from childhood through his first two years of college. Upon graduation, he sought and took my advice to take whatever job he could find with one of the NHL teams, hoping to someday move up within the club. He eventually landed a sales job that paid straight commission, where the risk of failure was entirely on him. However, his passion for ice hockey energized him to work with extraordinary vigor, and he succeeded beyond his employer's wildest expectations. He was promoted to a management job within his first year.

Mark followed a different dream. He joined the volunteer services group at his university, and spent the summer of his junior year rebuilding the humble dwellings of poor South Americans. This changed his whole perspective of the world. He described his time in South America as one of the most fulfilling in his young life. He desperately wanted to return through a two-year stint in the Peace Corps, but his father strongly urged him to find a professional job and begin paying off his student loans.

He came to me with this dilemma: Should he follow his passion and disappoint his father, or follow his father's wishes and give up his dream?

Are you surprised to learn that I told him to follow his dream? Mark's father's wishes and concerns were valid, but who would bear the direct and long-term negative consequences of this decision? Who would be left with unfulfilled dreams? Mark returned to South America, and with his father's blessing. His letters to me indicate that the experience was unforgettable and fascinating.

My consulting clients and the professional audiences I address articulate the issues differently. Their personal and work lives are considerably more complex. Any change could have a serious negative impact on their lifestyles, relationships with friends and family, and their own self-images. One corporate executive told me: "Sure, I would love to become a high school teacher, but look at the drop in income as well as the additional schooling I would need to qualify! My spouse would have to enter the work force, and we still might not be able to maintain our standard of living!"

I said, "At your stage of life, this opportunity may not come about again. Are you willing to live out your life without at least trying to make this dream happen?"

He accepted the challenge, quit his job, and entered school. The last time I heard from him he had no regrets, including the loss of his beloved BMW!

Two additional comments may help clarify and extend this perspective. The search for passion must be a lifelong quest. Passionate feelings about people, hobbies, and jobs may change over time as our needs and desires evolve. We must allow ourselves to seek new opportunities and to refocus our lives when necessary. If we do, there may be short-term negative consequences and long-term uncertainties. However, life with passion is worth the price!

Second, living a life filled with passion is contagious. It is likely to have a delightful impact on your family, friends, and coworkers. Some of your acquaintances may react with envy, probably because they have relinquished the pursuit of their own special dreams. However, those with talent and the determination to make the most of their lives will heed the call and join the passionate in their crusade for a fulfilling life!

Chapter 5

Performance, Jealousy, and Envy

In junior high school, when I began to actualize my abilities, I became passionate about learning, and my desire for new information was almost insatiable. My teachers and parents were quite pleased with this change, and their positive feedback energized my intellectual quest.

However, I didn't receive accolades from every quarter. There were students who viewed my performance with contempt, as if my success lessened them in some way. Fortunately, other students shared my enthusiasm for learning, and we competed with and admired each other.

Such experiences and their meanings were revealed to me slowly over a number of years. One memorable incident occurred at the national doctoral student consortium sponsored by the American Marketing Association. This event brings together students in graduate business programs from around the country to meet, listen, and talk with leading scholars in the fields of marketing and consumer behavior. As a doctoral student from a modest program, I viewed my invitation as an honor as well as an opportunity to interact with people whose names were engraved in my mind after years of reading their research articles.

I spent every session during the three-day conference in rapt attention as these academics revealed their perspectives of the field. I spoke up often, asked questions and addressed their musings. I made several friends among fellow students, and I still value these associations. However, a few students made disparaging remarks to me: "Why did you attend all the sessions and make all of those comments? Who are you trying to impress?"

I was taken aback. Was this small band of students right? Should I back off?

The more I pondered their remarks the more I disagreed with them. I was living life to the fullest and taking advantage of a rare opportunity. If they chose to be indifferent, it was their loss.

With this resolve, I entered professional life. While I had a few self-doubts and false starts, for the most part I pursued my work with all the energy and enthusiasm I could muster. My drive and subsequent performance allowed me to advance quickly within the academic community, both inside and outside my own university. I felt successful, and success felt good.

I was challenged again during my first administrative job. I had joined the faculty of a regionally known university after spending a year at a nationally ranked business school. I was very pleased to accept the position because of its mission, its student body, and its desire for greater prominence in the academic community. The dean of the business school, Al Clay, was particularly kind and generous, and made me feel welcome.

Not all the faculty viewed my hire in the same light. They expressed concern that people like me might change the culture of the university from its traditional roots. The values they embraced represented the status quo. Who was I, and others like me, to come in and mess up a good thing?

Their challenge bothered me, until I realized that their concern was for their own welfare, not the university's. The rules of the old system favored them, or at least left them alone to pursue their interests without interference. Although the new system required accountability and performance, which was valued by the larger community of scholars, to this group accountability and performance were foreign and formidable.

After two years, Dean Clay asked me to act as chair of the marketing department and help him implement the cultural change. Together with several other "chairs" and members of the faculty, we developed a solid strategic plan to re-engineer the school's approach to teaching and scholarship. We were certain it was time for change to keep in step with the business community we served, and worked diligently at the task for the next five years.

Our detractors did everything to undermine our efforts. Although they rarely voiced their concerns publicly, they carried on a kind of "jungle warfare." Office gossip was the primary weapon in their attempts to preserve "the old guard." Ultimately, they were unable to halt the forward movement of the institution, but they did succeed in making the changes more painful than necessary for everyone involved.

Unlike the man who married five times but divorced each spouse because she was selfish, I recognize my complicity in these situations. Very competitive and outgoing by nature, I was brutally honest with people who failed to do their jobs properly. This combination of traits made me visible in most public situations. I was a target for both admiration and disdain. I tolerated the negativity from certain peers when praise came from my superiors (parents, teachers, coaches, and bosses). However, as I matured, I began to realize that my performance could threaten individuals at all levels within the institution. It became clear that being good in ways which traditionally brought praise didn't always bear the same results in the adult world.

I began to explore the impact of this on people who operate in different organizational environments. I came across many examples in my consulting work but two, in particular, stand out. One involves Carin Porter, an executive with a prestigious Fortune-500 firm. I have worked with Carin for over 12 years, and found her to be one of the most capable and savvy business thinkers I've ever met. Self-educated and perceptive, she rose quickly in her career to the level of senior vice president before her 35th birthday.

People throughout the industry noticed her meteoric rise, and the top executive in her firm began to sing her praises to all who would listen. While this attention and her subsequent performance earned her the respect of many, it also threatened a contingent of professionals at or near her corporate level. Instead of confronting her directly with their fears, they used vicious gossip to discredit her. They also instructed their staffs to withdraw support of her work-related activities. The last thing they wanted to do was help her (or the firm) succeed!

A lesser person might have surrendered; especially as she was the only woman in the boardroom. However, her detractors failed to recognize Carin's intense desire to succeed, her passion, and the inherent ability she possessed. After several years and many difficult battles, she remains with the firm while most, if not all, of her detractors have been dismissed.

The second example is from the experiences of Bill McDonald. I've known Bill since our college days. He gives 100 percent to his professional life, and he has an uncanny ability to understand the subtle political nuances of corporate culture. He has worked for seven firms over the past twenty years, and his movements always resulted in higher pay, privilege, and position.

During this time, Bill learned that the combination of effort and ability often led to a high level of performance, which was noticed by his bosses as well as his peers. However, as his success and reputation grew, so did the number of detractors who felt threatened by him. As with Carin, these individuals used negativity and gossip in an attempt to thwart Bill's enormous presence.

Bill's reaction to their strategy changed over the years, as he gained insight into their behavior. At first, he viewed their vicious and underhanded tactics as personal attacks, requiring direct and immediate confrontation. Now he recognizes them for what they are — defense mechanisms against a level of performance that seem to be beyond their reach. Since quality organizations value success above talk, Bill knows that he will out last less competent rivals.

These rivals—were they motivated by envy, or was it jealousy that drove them? The American Heritage Dictionary (1982) describes envy as "a feeling of discontent and resentment aroused by another's desirable possessions or qualities, accompanied by a strong desire to have them for oneself." Jealousy, on the other hand, occurs when one is "fearful or wary of being supplanted, especially apprehensive of the loss of another's affection."

In the cases of Carin and Bill, it appears that their colleagues experienced both envy and jealousy. Their colleagues resented the actualization of their ability-performance nexus (Chapter 3), and felt that Carin or Bill was a threat to their corporate status. The defense mechanisms chosen to deal with these emotions were self- and other-destructive, and caused negative outcomes for all parties as well as their organizations.

Envy and jealousy only serve to reduce productivity, harm careers, and spoil working relationships within the adult world. Both Carin and Bill were forced to allocate precious time to defend their decisions and actions in order to adequately address the charges of their detractors. Also, their detractors spent precious time plotting and scheming to undermine Carin's or Bill's position. Significant amounts of energy that should have been dedicated to promoting the firms' interests were siphoned off to these tactics. Further, all parties experienced damage to their emotional well-being, to their careers, and, ultimately, to their quality of life.

To resolve the problems caused by envy and jealousy, we need to manage our responses to our own feelings as well as the feelings of others. Remember: Being tough depends upon who is in the room at the time. We can always find someone who outperforms us at least some of the time. Once we realize this, the next step is to avoid the negative actions that envy and jealousy evoke.

One way to do this is to work with successful individuals. Learn their success secrets. Our own performance will improve, and our reputations may be enhanced through association.

Managing others' reactions is difficult. Since those who suffer from envy and jealousy tend to view successful people in negative terms, their underhanded tactics often make direct and public confrontation ineffective. One alternative is to have one-to-one meetings with your detractors. Use these meetings to seek ways to negotiate a truce and, ultimately, create cooperative and mutually beneficial working relationships. "Keep your friends close and your enemies closer."

Not all criticism can be met with an opportunity. Some detractors do not merit it, due to their poor ability-performance nexus. However, we shouldn't fool ourselves that all detractors are incompetent, or that their underhandedness will be seen for what it is by those whose opinions we value. Mutually satisfying solutions allow all parties to meet their goals and advance their positions. In work and professional conflicts, this will simultaneously benefit the parent organization. If these efforts do not succeed, we must nonetheless remain focused and centered on meeting our own goal, and ignore the machinations of detractors.

Part 2: On Ability and Performance

Part 3: Managing Self and Others

*E*xample is not the main thing influencing others. It is the only thing.

—Albert Schweitzer

Part 3: On Managing Self and Others

Chapter 6

Mentors

My father was a good role model. He faced many obstacles in his personal and professional life, but was always able to overcome them for the sake of his family and his employer. My earliest recollections of him taught me a variety of lessons. The most memorable are: be an independent thinker; stand up for your rights; long-term success requires hard work; and be humble in the face of victory. I learned these values in the best possible way: by observing his actions.

When I was in high school, my father became my career mentor. He was a senior executive in a trade association located in Washington, DC, and he spent considerable time with professional managers from around the country. One of his responsibilities was to develop and promote educational and training opportunities for these managers. Because I showed an interest in the business world, he invited me to one of the events his firm sponsored.

The seminar truly transformed me. He introduced me to several people who went out of their way to talk to me about their jobs. I listened to the speakers, laughed at their opening remarks, and was impressed by their insights. On the drive home from this event, my father and I discussed the backgrounds of each individual whom I had heard or met. Their credentials were impressive, and I vowed to work hard in order to join their ranks one day.

As the years passed, my father continued to introduce me to a variety of people at his job. Each took the time to give me advice they believed was the key to their own success: marketing is the field to enter; make sure you get your MBA; start your career in a developing industry that is experiencing growth; and so on. I agreed with much of their advice and followed many of their recommendations, hoping to emulate their accomplishments.

One person, in particular, was especially influential. The man was a business professor in an urban university, and he regularly was hired by my father to give lectures and training seminars. He was soft spoken and kind, but also direct. "If you want the life I lead, you need to stay in school until you earn the Ph.D. degree."

I asked my father's opinion of this advice. He believed it was sound. He had met and hired many academics during his career, and thought they had the best of all possible worlds. University life was stimulating and prestigious, and the consulting and public speaking opportunities for the successful ones were quite lucrative. He strongly urged me to follow this man's lead.

I entered college guided by several of these insights, worked hard as a student, and often applied my newfound knowledge to part-time jobs. Fortunately, two men recognized my ability-performance nexus, and they provided encouragement as well as direction.

One of these mentors was my original martial arts teacher, Dale Tompkins, who was about ten years older than I. Dale was aggressively building his karate school and needed dedicated instructors to expand his program. I demonstrated an ability to teach as well as a passion for martial arts, and quickly became one of his top instructors.

During my years in his employ, Dale taught me many lessons about how to be a successful entrepreneur. His business increased at least five-fold over this time, and I was encouraged to apply my blossoming knowledge of management to his programs. Some ideas succeeded, others failed, but the opportunity to apply the latest academic thinking within this growing business allowed me to develop my leadership skills. Dale was always generous with praise as well as financial rewards for these efforts, and these allowed me to explore other aspects of the world with confidence.

The marketing professor mentioned earlier had a similar impact on my life. I met Paul Bloom when I was a junior in college, and he decided to be my academic career mentor. He guided me in selection of courses, recommended me for a scholarship in my last year as an undergraduate, and paved the way for my admission into the graduate program.

The courses Professor Bloom taught were the most critical to my future as a researcher and teacher. His classes explored the impact, both positive and negative, of marketing upon society. We discussed issues of regulation, and the roles played by government agencies such as the Federal Trade Commission. I left these courses believing that businesses needed to rise above the pure profit motive and consider the larger societal responsibilities. Without this paradigm, I might never have found an appropriate outlet for my passion within academia.

Men and women who significantly influenced my life include other coaches, teachers, and friends who took a special interest in my personal and/or professional development. In the best of these relationships, we both benefited financially, interpersonally, and in terms of career growth. I would not have achieved as much success in my life without these mentors.

To be a mentor is to be an influential force in the life of another person. Typically, the "mentee" is a younger and less experienced person, one who is talented and eager to learn. The mentor helps the mentee understand critical aspects of the world, and provides the context in which to shape a portion of his or her ability-performance nexus. The mentee opens himself to the ideas, philosophies, and directions provided by the mentor, often placing his future in his mentor's hands. In many respects, this is an awesome responsibility for the mentor and a vulnerable place for the mentee.

To be a successful mentor, one must recognize and accept all that the role of mentor entails. Next, the mentor must look at the costs and benefits of mentoring. One must ask: Is mentoring this person more trouble than it is worth? Beyond the good feeling associated with helping another person, how may I expect to be rewarded?

The best mentoring relationships are mutually beneficial, enhancing the personal and/or professional lives of both parties.

The mentee also must assess the mentoring relationship realistically. He must ask himself: What do I hope to gain from this association? Am I willing to cede valuable portions of my life to this person? Just as important is an assessment of what the mentee brings to the relationship. What can I give to this relationship that is truly valuable to the mentor? Is this value sustainable for as long as the association is expected to last?

Most of these pairings do not occur with such explicit and articulated aims. They develop slowly, like most important relationships, and their meanings often are revealed belatedly. Coaches, teachers, bosses, family, friends—any of these can fill the role of mentor; although the mentee typically is unaware of what they give in return, a conscious process of search and selection on both sides is more likely to end in positive growth for all parties.

Due to my upbringing and positive experiences, I often sought out successful individuals as mentors. While a young professor I sought the best scholars in my areas of interest, talked to them about our mutual research agendas and offered to do much of the unpleasant tasks ("grunt" work) to produce publishable scholarship. Some were put off, others were polite, but the few who responded with enthusiasm became valuable collaborators as well as friends.

My bias towards the long-term benefits of mentoring should not suggest that these relationships are without their problems and pitfalls. Opposite sex mentoring, especially when the mentee is female, requires caution to ensure that the woman's integrity does not become the topic of office gossip. But it is essential that capable women in our workforce receive mentoring opportunities in what often are male-dominated professions.

A second problem associated with office politics involves the potential for loss of status of the mentor, who may even leave the firm. When this occurs, those who are strong supporters may share in the "fall from grace," often testing the true loyalty of the mentee.

A third problem involves ending the mentoring relationship. In the best cases, both the mentor and the mentee experience growth and the relationship flourishes. However, there are occasions when the mentee fails to actualize his or her ability-performance nexus, or eventually exceeds the ability-performance nexus of the mentor. When this occurs, a graceful exit is necessary through an honest and open appraisal of the relationship by both parties. The intent is to create some professional distance, yet salvage what is left of the working relationship. Otherwise, the "breakup" remains forever incomplete, with one or both parties left feeling confused, bitter, or angry. Such an ending does not foster trust in future professional interactions.

The lesson I learned is that most of us, regardless of the good and helpful intentions of our parents, must find role models to emulate in various aspects of our adult lives. This process typically occurs without conscious thought; we find people within our environments whom we like and respect, and the feeling is mutual. Some of these relationships are beneficial for both parties over the long run, while others fail to live up to their potential. To increase the success rate, one must consciously seek and find individuals whose abilities and long-term goals are good matches in ways that are mutually beneficial. Honesty and trust are essential to make the most of these relationships through their useful lives. Sadly, many of these relationships are temporary, and we must have the courage, insight, and integrity to move on when they no longer serve their purpose. We must do so in ways that preserve those portions of the association that remain valuable.

Chapter 7

Authority and Accountability

When I think of truly great leaders, I focus on individuals whom I have observed firsthand in leadership roles. Important attributes such as "charismatic," "visionary," and "commanding," fail to capture the day-to-day qualities that make an effective leader.

Among those individuals who represent leadership at its finest is a business-school dean, Al Clay, whom I had the honor of serving during one of my tours of duty as a university professor. In addition to all the attributes noted above, Al was honest with the faculty and they knew he was trustworthy. His genuine respect for the institution and all who worked there inspired our appreciation for the school and for one another. He established clear performance standards and saw that these standards were enforced without bias. And, he was unafraid to use his strengths and admit his limitations.

Al and I first met when I sought a job on his faculty. This was the tenth university I'd visited. It had become a drill, moving from interview to interview. Al Clay was the first dean who took a genuine interest in me. He helped me examine my career goals, shared his vision of the institution, and honestly assessed how the two intersected or failed to intersect. Putting aside his own daily routine and responsibilities for an entire afternoon, Al gave me a personal tour of the campus he loved. Thus, I had the opportunity to see the university through his eyes, and felt welcomed and valued.

Beth Hirschman is one of the most recognized individuals in business education today, and she exhibits leadership without a formal position of power. Admired widely as one of the most accomplished scholars in the field of marketing, Beth is the author of an impressive array of articles, books, and conference papers. During her career she often questioned the direction of our collective thinking, and her work has expanded the boundaries of the discipline.

Beth has mentored dozens of emerging scholars throughout her career, helping them assess their own value within the field and encouraging them to take bold steps. She leads by example, and is selfless in her willingness to advance the reputation of the rising stars around her. When she recently received a lifetime achievement award for her contribution to the discipline, her acceptance speech was filled with references to those who mentored her as well as those to whom she has been mentor. In her view, mentors and mentees are equally essential to her career growth as a successful professional.

Such individuals are the exception. Most of us are subject to the whims of people in superior positions who are unable or unwilling to lead. Here are two examples.

The first, a man, was a dean who I met early in my university service. He was new to the job, having transferred from another institution, and he began his tenure by interviewing each of us to determine our status and long-term goals. I was impressed by this initial interest. Later, it became apparent that the faculty assessment he performed so diligently was never used to determine the critical needs and strategic directions of the business school.

Instead, this dean pursued personal goals and objectives. Some faculty members assumed that these were the results of negotiations with the higher administration. Then several members of the faculty met in a public forum to express concern that the dean was ignoring our role in the planning process. Despite these discussions, nothing changed. Over time, as the dean became increasingly isolated from our views, he lost our respect. He left the position a few years later, virtually without internal support.

Another dean was a man of rare vision and excellent insights into how a university might change in order to meet the challenges of the twenty-first century. His combination of talent, accomplishments, vision, and charisma seemed to assure us of a very positive future.

Sadly, these traits were not enough to ensure his success. As soon as he took office he began a campaign of publicly belittling the faculty. According to many reliable sources, he regularly referred to us as "handicapped" and "unmarketable." This implied that he was saddled with a faculty who were without merit. He denied such claims as mere office gossip fed by fear of a new and progressive leader. But the result was that few among us were willing to follow his plans for change. Within a year he was forced to resign the deanship and return to teaching. Most cheered this removal but, in truth, both sides lost time, resources, and the opportunity to shape a better future for the school.

We often seek as leaders individuals who possess certain "ideal" characteristics. Far too often, leadership positions are filled with little regard to how the leaders plan to actualize their potential. The authority that comes with leadership must be coupled with a sincere interest in the goals and aspirations of those who are expected to follow. This is especially true in a loosely aligned institution such as a university.

Leadership is epitomized by mentor relationships that advance the careers of both leaders and followers, as well as the organization's mission. This approach is likely to create a positive force among employees sustainable over the long term.

A compassionate leadership style does not preclude accountability or the exercise of strong leadership. At a recent meeting, the keynote speaker, not from academia, bemoaned the endless series of meetings conducted in her firm to gain acceptance for strategic decisions. She concluded her talk by saying "Consensus is a poor excuse for a lack of leadership."

The message here is that leaders must be willing to make tough, occasionally unpopular, decisions in the face of convincing evidence that such decisions best serve the interest of the organization.

As boards of regents, or directors, feel increasing pressure from external publics for radical reform, most institutions of higher education as well as business and nonprofit organizations demand greater accountability from employees. Tenure, teaching loads, and the primacy of research are all coming under increasing scrutiny.

Most of us embrace the status quo rather than search for opportunities to build a better educational system. The number of academic leaders who continue to accept less than we are capable of accomplishing is shocking. They have chosen the path of less resistance, perhaps out of fear of alienating their faculty and becoming less globally popular.

An appropriate alternative may be to forge new alliances with diverse constituencies in such a way as to meet our needs as well as their increasingly influential set of expectations. This may require a reward system that asks us to seek continuous quality improvements in all aspects of our jobs (i.e., teaching, research, and service). This system would require academic leaders to recognize the importance of individual and group performance over the traditional measures of status, like rank or seniority. More drastic measures, including the removal of unproductive faculty, may also be required.

True leadership requires leaders to construct their vision for the organization within a humane context which considers the long-term interests and aspirations of those expected to follow. This does not preclude leaders from exercising strong leadership or enforcing accountability. Quite the contrary. Good leaders, like good mentors, recognize the importance of a symbiotic relationship between themselves and their followers, but they also recognize that these relationships must serve the needs of the larger collective or organization.

Part 3: On Managing Self and Others

Chapter 8

Multiple Roles/Multiple Selves

L ife was easy when we were infants. We were born with great need, but little was expected of us. Our days were filled with eating, sleeping, and eliminating. Uncomplicated.

Within months, demands were made on us. Family members were to make demands: smile now, eat now, speak now, walk now, and a host of subtle requests. Gradually, these expectations mold us into the adults we are today, people who play multiple roles, who have multiple lives.

P.J., my nine-year-old son, is aware of his multiple roles. He has responsibilities as a son, brother, grandson, and nephew. At school, he is a student, peer, friend, and teammate. Each of these roles may provide him with some joy, but they also place demands on his ability-performance nexus. He is expected to be polite, share, sit quietly, raise his hand, complete homework assignments, achieve high grades on quizzes and tests, hustle at games. Whether P.J. wants to or not, he is compelled to perform.

Let's consider a more complete, adult example. Melissa, then a female graduate student, stopped by my office to chat about fond memories of undergraduate days more than five years past, and how she yearned to be in a "learning environment" once again. Caught up in her exuberance, I asked her to tell me more about her life.

Her first child was now a year old, she said, and she was exercising hard to get back to marathon-running physical condition. And, she had just been promoted by her employer to a position that required longer hours and more travel.

I was incredulous. "You have an infant at home, a demanding job, and a grueling physical regimen. How can you possibly do all that, much less add two graduate courses a semester?"

Without hesitation, she announced, "I'm a good time manager!"

Multiple roles and multiple selves are evident in the lifestyle of the typical faculty member. Teaching activities spill over into our research time. Summers are spent catching up on research projects we neglected in favor of meeting students' demand for additional office hours. When business offices around the country are winding down for the holiday season, we are busy grading piles of exam papers.

Then there are service requirements, from the university community as well as our professional organizations. These increase as we become more successful and rise within the profession; there is always one more paper to draft or revise. The tasks seem endless, time consuming, and quite often without tangible rewards.

Successful faculty, as well as successful professionals, would probably agree that time management is required to meet the demands of daily living. However, the most skilled person can do no more than manage time. None is capable of creating more.

Carin Porter, a successful executive in a global company, has unrelenting demands on her time. Technology is the tool through which she manages her time. Since she frequently jets from one locale to another, as soon as her plane lands and before she leaves the airport, Carin checks her cell phone for messages or calls her home office. When she reaches the visiting office, she finds a pile of faxes waiting. Through e-mail she connects with subsidiaries all over the world. Carin's pace is steady from 6 A.M. to midnight. Despite these professional demands, she is able to maintain a satisfying personal life.

More complex than time management but equally important is another tool: self-management. Time management requires us to think in blocks of time. Self-management requires us to consider our unique personal needs. With *time management,* we prioritize according to urgency. With *self-management,* we acknowledge the long-term importance of these demands to our selves. This is important since, as we age, we tend to increase the number of roles we play.

Self-management of multiple roles is a serious problem among the baby boom generation. Many boomers tenaciously hold onto the trappings of their youth. They also balance the increasingly complex role of a child who cares for elderly parents with the role of parent who coaches Little League, tutors children, and provides a bus service around town. These activities and roles often are in addition to those we must manage for our professional lives.

There are two essential ingredients to successful self-management: willingness to accept new roles, and the ability to shed old roles that no longer are fulfilling. Adding roles is far easier than shedding roles. Adding generally is accompanied by gain. Shedding often means the loss of something once valuable.

Many remarkable women suffer enormously when they have to choose between relinquishing the role of mother or the role of successful professional. If they stay at home, they lose opportunities to advance their careers, to interact with peers, and to experience the satisfaction of completing difficult tasks. If they return to work after childbirth, they miss sharing their children's earliest experiences, as well as important bonding.

Often the result is guilt or fear. One working mother complained: "When my son wakes up at night, the first name he calls out is the nanny's."

Her dilemma can be solved if she establishes a priority system and ranks her roles so that she allocates her time accordingly. One person may define the roles of spouse and parent as primary, with secondary ranks being the roles of working professional and child to elderly parents. Other activities—coach for Little League, long-distance runner, musician—may be tertiary.

As a result of establishing a priority system, you might decide that you are no longer interested in attending local school board meetings or preparing the monthly spaghetti dinner at church.

We must be willing to honestly assess the long-term value of each self to the total person we are or aspire to be. This process must be ongoing and revisited continually throughout our lives. As we evolve, the responsibilities of each self may increase or decrease in significance, and new selves may emerge.

We all know people who spread themselves thin because they do not prioritize their roles. The underlying problem may be failure to shed roles that no longer are useful. Or it may be failure to organize roles hierarchically and allocate time accordingly. Either way, they are confused about priorities, in conflict with important others, and feel stressed, angry, or guilty.

Time management, while valuable, has limitations. Given that we all have the same number of hours in a day, self-management is essential.

It requires us to regularly take a critical look at each of the selves that make up who we are, and decide which are significant. Our individual hierarchy should then be our guide in determining how time is allocated to each role and its responsibilities.

Part 3: On Managing Self and Others

Part 4: Relationships

Many hands and hearts and minds generally contribute to anyone's notable achievements.

—Walt Disney

Part 4: On Relationships

Chapter 9

Love, Marriage, and Compatibility

New love is one of the few times that our lives are con-sumed with passion. Our desire to be with our love interest eclipses many of our mundane needs, causing us to abandon some of the role requirements of our other selves. We share our innermost secrets with this person, experienc-ing deeply felt intimacy. We feel vulnerable, yet safe in their arms and in their hearts.

The first time I was in love was in my senior year of high school, and I was ready to experience a more "mature" rela-tionship. The girl had been a friend for several years. Once we discovered our adoration for one another we became in-separable, and rescheduled our lives to be together as much as possible. In time schooling, hobbies, friends, and other in-terests merged so that we seemed more like a unit than two distinct individuals.

As we matured into young adults, our important goals and values began to take different directions. Her primary passions were art, music, and athletics, while mine were business, politics, and athletics. She wanted a simple life with few material possessions, and I desired a family and all the trappings of middle-class success. Our initial passion and hope for enduring love were unable to keep us together.

Our breakup wasn't easy. When we both realized that our relationship was over, much of our lives were firmly intertwined. As we sought to unravel our union, we found that family, friends, and coworkers were affected significantly.

My mother had passed away a few years earlier and her mother had become my substitute mom. Since I spent most holidays with her family, our breakup meant losing them, too. I was relinquishing one self, and the impact on many others was apparent.

Few among us recognize the process by which we move from the passion of new love to the commitment of marriage, and the impact this change in status has on our various selves. On our wedding day, we simultaneously become husband/wife, son/daughter-in-law, brother/sister-in-law, uncle/aunt, and with these new roles we have new rights and responsibilities. Many of us also become father/mother, a self that has enormous implications throughout our lives.

The cumulative effect of these changes on our overall sense of self goes beyond the roles and may affect how we define ourselves, even in the workplace. I once read "The quality of our marriage has the ability to cause 90% of our happiness or sorrow."

We rarely understand the ramifications of our decision to create a more lasting union with a man or woman, or the decision not to do so. Except in the well-publicized cases of "marrying for money," we often fail to acknowledge that our choices in marriage can facilitate or detract from our ability-performance nexus.

A client of mine met his wife in high school. To avoid separation, they chose to attend the same college. After dating each other exclusively for over five years, they decided to marry soon after graduation.

Many friends, certain that this couple would regret not "playing the field" in their younger years, predicted eventual doom for their relationship. But my client and his wife spent countless hours discussing their hopes, fears, and aspirations. These conversations led to joint decisions about their lives, and they worked together to achieve mutual goals.

They took turns supporting each other through graduate school. After their first child was born, they each took a month's vacation from their jobs to adjust to parenthood, and took turns as the stay-at-home parent. Neither their careers nor their family life suffered, and they were able to avoid the turmoil, guilt, and other negative emotions sometimes associated with this important rite-of-passage. Both advanced quickly at their jobs, but they continue to devote most of their leisure time to family activities.

A female colleague was a doctoral student at another university as I was studying for my Ph.D. The life of a graduate student at that level is very hectic. It is filled with endless books and scholarly articles to read, papers to write, and discussions involving both activities. Most graduate students work late into the night to accommodate the schedules of their professors and peers.

My friend joined the graduate program following a stellar performance as an undergraduate at a major state university. In her last year of undergraduate school she married, and her husband launched his career in business when she began graduate school.

Their relationship deteriorated. He wanted to spend time with her in the evenings and on weekends when he was home from work; she needed this time for her studies.

After two years he persuaded her that it was the "right time" to start a family. When the child was born, the responsibility for the baby's care was left to her and her work suffered. After two more years fighting about whose career was the greater priority, the couple split up—a clear example of "irreconcilable differences."

Divorce used to be considered taboo. It was thought to tarnish a person's reputation. Today we view divorce as inevitable in half of all marriages. Even so, we rarely understand the impact of a prosperous or failed union on our sense of self or on our ability-performance nexus.

One might come away with the impression that success or failure depends on whether each spouse's goals and responsibilities are treated equally. This may be true, but it does not tell the whole story. It's my opinion that the most important element in a successful and fulfilling relationship is the compatibility of a couple's life goals. It was the relative harmony or disharmony of their married selves that facilitated or inhibited the personal and professional achievements of each couple.

The experience of new love is one of the most intense and satisfying of our lives. But for love to become a fulfilling and lasting union, a couple must uphold the same goals, ambitions, and behaviors.

People mature and encounter new ideas, people, and events. To remain compatible, we must continue to discuss and modify our personal and professional lives with our significant other.

Chapter 10

Treatment of Other People

My father believed that when children were able and were permitted to work, they should earn enough to cover their own entertainment expenses, school books and, eventually, car insurance. Thus, I got a "worker's permit" at age fourteen, and began a series of low-wage positions.

I learned that not all jobs treated people with the kindness my friends and family had shown me. In some jobs, coworkers and I received respect and appreciation for our efforts. In others, we were ignored, taken advantage of, and even harmed. Most positions had aspects of both.

After working as a paperboy and locker-room attendant, I took a part-time position as a busboy in a restaurant near my high school. I worked three or four nights a week, and was paid a dollar an hour plus a portion of the waitresses' tips. The employees treated each other with respect unless someone did substandard work. Then, peer pressure caused that person to perform to standards.

Unlike the attitude of coworkers, restaurant management personnel rarely spoke to any of us unless they were angry. Then, the tones and words they used were harsh. Only once did a manager approach me with civility, and the reason soon became clear. The manager wanted me to clean up a customer's vomit in the women's bathroom.

My next position was as retail clerk in the local store of a regional chain. I would no longer be knee-deep in people's leftover food. I began work eagerly, since several students that I knew from high school worked there. On my first day, I made a large error that cost the firm almost $100. The manager could have fired me; he could have taken the money out of my wages. Instead, he chose to explain my mistake and gave me a second chance. My subsequent hard work was rewarded with better pay, special responsibilities, and greater decision-making authority.

The first time I was on the other side of the power equation I was a karate instructor. I had trained in the martial arts for about two years, and the "sensei" (teacher) recognized both my desire and ability to instruct. It was an honor to be entrusted with the physical safety of students, and I enjoyed every aspect of this job, especially meeting new people, demonstrating techniques, and watching my students grow within the discipline.

Over time I found that I had earned the respect of students, almost to the point of "hero worship." I had seen a certain amount of abuse of this status within and without the karate school, and vowed to give my students the opportunity to develop to their fullest potential in a safe, positive, yet demanding environment.

Probably the most confusing job I held was as an instructor of marketing during graduate school. The treatment I received from two different groups was markedly different. The undergraduate business students were very similar to the aspiring martial artists—interested in learning, trusting, responsive and respectful. The full-time faculty, however, often was discourteous to me in my role as graduate student. Many of them were untenured assistant professors, burdened by the "publish or perish" dictum, and under tremendous pressure to perform in their jobs or face dismissal. Some of their frustration and anger was taken out on the doctoral students, who were the "next dog down." We were belittled, asked to accomplish ridiculous amounts of work in short periods of time, and given virtually no positive feedback.

As I advanced in my academic career, I witnessed a variety of attitudes from faculty toward students. Some professors went to great lengths to furnish students with a meaningful academic experience within a context of mutual respect and support. But there also were faculty who looked upon students as intellectually inferior beings as well as impediments that divert them from their "real" work (i.e., research).

An accomplished management scholar admitted he organized his office to discourage students from staying long. He bragged that no student had remained in his office for longer than ten minutes!

I have talked to hundreds of managers about how they treat their employees. Curious to learn about individuals who occupy prominent positions in their customers' eyes, I asked about the person who answers their telephones: "What kind of training does she or he receive? How is she or he managed?"

A typical answer is, "That person has a low-level job that requires little attention or encouragement by a manager."

My response is, "To your customers and all those who

initially contact your firm, this person represents all they know about you. Can you afford not to train the person in this important position?"

Another discussion revolves around the best and the worst employees in a firm. Most managers feel that the best employees are self-motivated and successful at actualizing their ability-performance nexus. Thus, the managers spend much of their time dealing with "problem children."

My question is: "You spend your time with under-performers and none with the overachievers. Your best will probably remain motivated without your attention, but will they stay with your firm?"

Managers agree that keeping their best employees is a difficult challenge.

In business, although the Golden Rule has merit, "doing unto others as we would have them do unto us" may not be enough. We might consider treating all people with the same respect, encouragement, and concern for their future as we do for the special individuals in our lives.

Such an approach does not preclude the enforcement of accountability. Unconditional acceptance may exist within families, but other relationships are based on some performance-based expectations. Consistent with the concept of "tough love" that parents use with children in crisis, holding people accountable for their failure to perform adequately is appropriate. We must also recognize the need to provide recognition and reward to those who meet or exceed our expectations. Neglect, even benign neglect, will serve to worsen, not improve our relationships and the performance of those with whom we have significant contact.

*N*ine-tenths of wisdom consists in being wise in time.

–Theodore Roosevelt

Pearls Along The Path

Epilogue: Lessons Learned

All relationships involve one or more of the characteristics discussed in these pages: Expectation; Performance; Comparison, Evaluation. We need to recognize that most individuals with whom we form personal or professional relationships expect us to meet certain goals or satisfy certain needs. Some of these expectations are explicit, others are implied, but we should be fully aware of what they are before we commit to their pursuit.

Additionally, we need to evaluate the extent to which reciprocity is involved: Are we getting something of equal or greater value in return for what is expected of us?

Regarding performance, it is rare when the mere presence of native ability ensures success. An additional and necessary ingredient is effort, and not just effort but effort of the highest order. For some of us working hard is second nature. The rest of us need to engage in pursuits that we are passionate about in order to give our all.

Comparison involves the inevitable examination of what we do in relation to relevant others. In some sense, we are in a "catch-22," If we fail to perform at an exceptional level, we may be seen as failures by ourselves as well as those around us. But if we excel, we are likely to be subjected to jealousy and envy and all the subsequent problems associated with these. Unless we establish our own explicit standards we will continuously be disappointed since there will always be someone who can achieve more than us on any given playing field.

Evaluation explores how individuals in superior positions (often positions of power) motivate, judge, and direct those over whom they have authority. How people are treated in such circumstances ranges from respect and concern to neglect and affront. Although true leadership requires that we hold people accountable for their performance, this must be done within a positive and encouraging environment that allows all parties to meet their goals.

Life can be lived more passionately if you discover and pursue your passions with vigor; if you set your own performance standards; if you compete against yourself rather than others; if you hold the people around you accountable for their actions, but also treat them with dignity and respect.

Thanks for allowing me to share with you the pearls I've picked up along my path. Let me know how you are doing along your path. (ronaldpaulhill@msn.com).

About the Author

Ronald Paul Hill, Ph.D., an internationally recognized teacher, consultant, and author of nearly 100 scholarly publications, began his teaching career as a martial arts instructor. Currently a university professor and Dean of the Dr. Robert B. Pamplin, Jr. School of Business Administration at the University of Portland, Oregon, he has served on the faculties of Cornell University, George Washington University, University of Maryland, The American University, and Villanova University.

Dr. Hill's scholarly work involves topics such as marketing management, advertising, health care, consumer behavior, and business ethics. Outlets include Journal of Marketing Research, Journal of Consumer Research, Journal of Advertising, Journal of Public Policy & Marketing, Journal of Consumer Affairs, Journal of Business Research, Journal of Health Care Marketing, Marketing Letters, Psychology and

Marketing, and Journal of Purchasing and Materials Management.

Dr. Hill is a member of the Association for Consumer Research, the American Council on Consumer Interests, the American Academy of Advertising, the American Marketing Association, and the honor societies of BETA GAMMA SIGMA, PHI KAPPA PHI, and PHI ETA SIGMA.

Dr. Hill has provided professional consultation to a number of associations, nonprofit organizations and major corporations including AT&T, Honeywell, and Cadillac. These activities include: market determination and segmentation, market needs assessment via focus groups and survey research, evaluations of market potential, audits of promotional methods, and strategy analyses. He also has presented marketing theory, strategy, and application as well as provided sales training to corporate and association audiences, and he has provided expert commentary to local and national media, including CNN and the Washington Post, on a variety of consumer behavior and marketing strategy issues.

Dr. Hill currently resides in Portland, Oregon with his wife Noel, his sons Paul and P.J., and their dog, Buddy.

Publications

Ronald Paul Hill, Ph.D. - with Julie Ozanne and Newell Wright (1998), "Juvenile Delinquents' Use of Consumption as Cultural Resistance: Implications for Juvenile Reform Programs and Public Policy," Journal of Public Policy & Marketing, 17 (Fall), 185-196.

_____- With Renya Reed (1998), "The Process of Becoming Homeless: An Investigation of Families in Poverty," Journal of Consumer Affairs, 32 (2), 320-332.

_____- With Cathy Goodwin (1998), "Commitment To Physical Fitness: Commercial Influences On long-term Healthy Consumer Behaviors," Social Marketing Quarterly, 4 (Spring), 68-83.

_____- With Debra Stephens, (1997) "Impoverished Consumers and Consumer Behavior: The Case of AFDC Mothers," Journal of Macromarketing, 17 (Fall), 32-48.

_____- With Cathy Goodwin and Michael Mayo (1997), "Salesperson Loss of A Major Account: A Qualitative Analysis," Journal of Business Research, 40 (October), 167-180.

_____- With Jane Keffer (1997), "An Ethical Approach to Lobbying Activities of Businesses in the United States," Journal of Business Ethics, 16 (12/13), 1371-1379.

_____- With Jim Gentry, Pat Kennedy, and Katherine Paul (1995), "The Vulnerability of Those Grieving the Death of a Loved One: Implications for Public Policy," Journal of Public Policy & Marketing, 14 (Spring), 128-142.

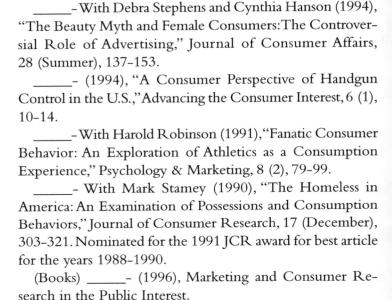

_____ – With Debra Stephens and Cynthia Hanson (1994), "The Beauty Myth and Female Consumers: The Controversial Role of Advertising," Journal of Consumer Affairs, 28 (Summer), 137-153.

_____ – (1994), "A Consumer Perspective of Handgun Control in the U.S.," Advancing the Consumer Interest, 6 (1), 10-14.

_____ – With Harold Robinson (1991), "Fanatic Consumer Behavior: An Exploration of Athletics as a Consumption Experience," Psychology & Marketing, 8 (2), 79-99.

_____ – With Mark Stamey (1990), "The Homeless in America: An Examination of Possessions and Consumption Behaviors," Journal of Consumer Research, 17 (December), 303-321. Nominated for the 1991 JCR award for best article for the years 1988-1990.

(Books) _____ – (1996), Marketing and Consumer Research in the Public Interest.

Consulting Activities

Provision of professional consultation to a number of associations, nonprofit organizations and major corporations. Current and former clients include: AT&T Technology Systems, Sallie Mae (Student Loan Marketing Association), National Association of Home Builders, American Leprosy Foundation, Westat, Inc., Association of Trial Lawyers of America, Mainstream, Inc., Physician's Pharmaceutical Services, Honeywell, Smart House, Saatchi & Saatchi (Tylenol/ Kaiser Permanente accounts), DMB&B (DeVille/Cadillac account).

Speeches

Presented marketing theory and application as well as provided sales training to corporate and association audiences. Recent groups include: National Education Association, American Society of Association Executives, National Limousine Association, Student Loan Marketing Association, Physician's Pharmaceutical Services, PRC Inc., Institute of Real Estate Management, Specialty Advertising Counselors of Delaware Valley, Premier Fabric, Trim, and Fiber, and Promotional Products Association International.

Media Interviews

Provided expert commentary to local and national media on a variety of consumer behavior and marketing strategy issues. Interviewers include: World Net (broadcast internationally through USIA), WTTG, WWDC, WRQX, WJLA, and the Washington Post in Washington, DC, WMCA and WNBC in New York, NY, WMWS in Miami, FL, WTKN in Pittsburgh, PA, WHYY in Philadelphia, PA, Lincoln Star-Journal in Lincoln, NE, Chicago Tribune in Chicago, IL, KATU, KPTV, KGW, KXL, KEWS, KOIN, KBOO, KPDX, KEX, KINK, Eugene Register-Guard, Oregon Business, Columbian, and the Oregonian in Portland, OR/Vancouver, WA, Mutual Broadcasting Network, National Public Radio, Post/Newsweek TV, Cable News Network, and American Journal.

Community And Volunteer Service

United Nations Speakers Bureau Human Rights Speaker, 1998-Present

Ad Hoc Committee on Downtown Portland Homeless Youth Services Committee Member, 1998

Oregon DMV Privatization Study Advisory Committee Committee Member, 1997-1998

Morrison Center for Abused and Neglected Children Board of Directors, 1996-1999, Volunteer, 1996-1997

Community Action Agency of Delaware County Strategic Planning Consultant, 1994-1996

Saint Gabriel's School for Juvenile Felons Life Skills Consultant, 1991

Missionaries of Charity Shelter for Homeless Women and Children Volunteer 1989-1990